TopReaders

How Does It Work?

Denise Ryan

Contents

How do machines, instruments,
and tools work? You can find out
how things work in this book.

Bicycle

You push a bike's pedals with your feet to make it go forward. You steer with the handlebars. Rubber tires grip the ground as you go.

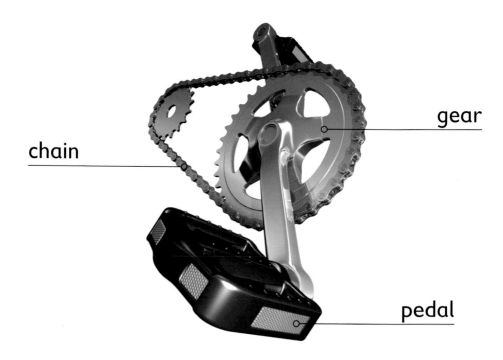

chain

gear

pedal

Pedals turn gears that are attached to a chain. The chain then turns the back wheel.

handlebars

rubber
tire

back
wheel

front wheel

pedal

Train

Trains run on electricity . They have streamlined bodies to move easily through the air. The driver controls the train from the engine as it speeds along the rails.

car passengers

Passengers travel in the cars, which are pulled by the engine.

electric cables

streamlined body

controls

Windmill

The blades of a windmill are turned by the wind. Wind energy powers moving parts inside the windmill.

Power from this windmill is used to pump water from nearby.

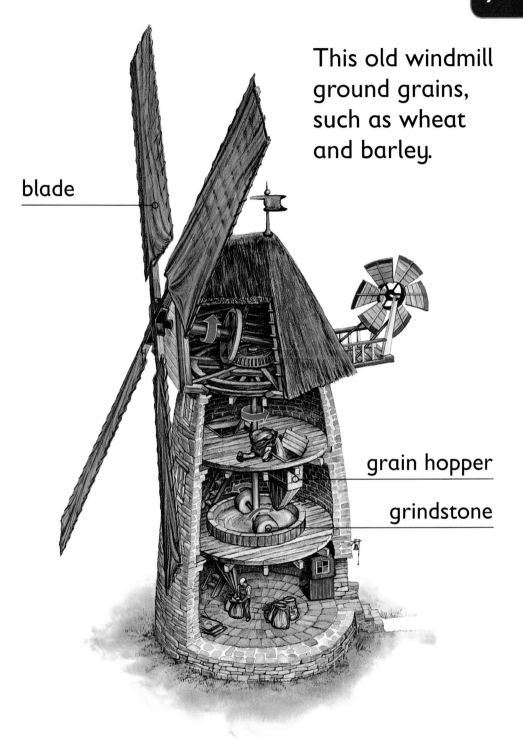

This old windmill ground grains, such as wheat and barley.

blade

grain hopper

grindstone

Clock

Clocks measure the time in hours, minutes, and seconds. The time is shown on the clock's face.

The pendulum of this clock swings every second. It drives the gears, which move the minute and hour hands.

hour hand

clock face

minute hand

pendulum

This electric clock shows us the time as a digital display.

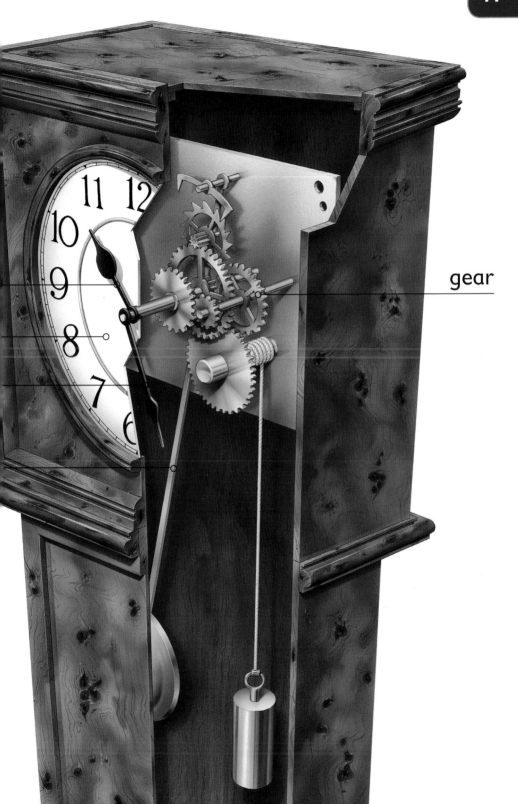

gear

Vacuum Cleaner

Vacuum cleaners help us to clean our homes. A powerful flow of air sucks up dirt and dust, then traps it inside a dust bag.

dust bag

motor

Dirt ends up here.

fan

The motor drives a spinning fan. This sucks air and dust through the long hose.

Dirt travels up the hose.

Dirt is sucked in here.

Microwave Oven

Microwave ovens use radio waves to cook food very quickly. A turntable inside spins around so that the food will cook more evenly.

You set the cooking time on the control panel and read it on the display.

display

turntable

control panel

Concrete Mixer

These large trucks have drums that mix and pour concrete. Concrete is used to make buildings and sidewalks.

drum   curved blades

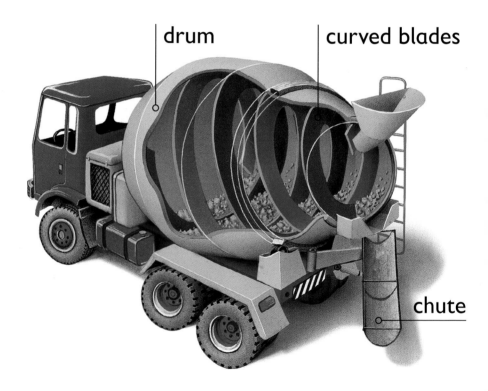

chute

As the drum turns, curved blades mix the concrete inside and push it into a chute.

Hot-air Balloon

Hot-air balloons rise because the hot air inside the balloon is lighter than the cooler air outside.

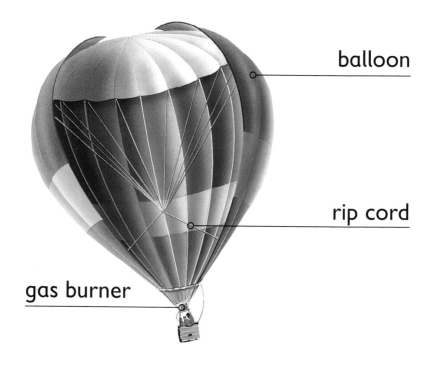

balloon

rip cord

gas burner

A gas burner heats the air inside. A rip cord lets the hot air out so the balloon can sink.

 climbing

 diving

 turning

Hang Glider

A hang-glider pilot leaps from the top of a cliff into the air. The glider has a single wing, which can climb, dive, and turn.

control bar

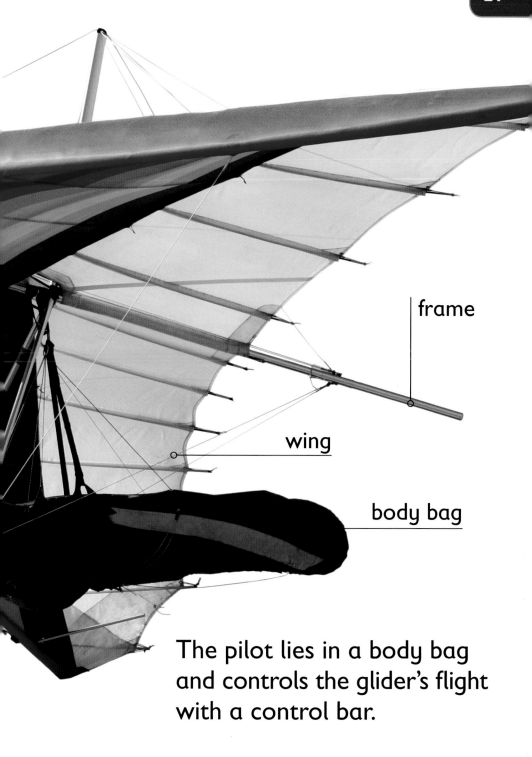

frame

wing

body bag

The pilot lies in a body bag and controls the glider's flight with a control bar.

Airplane

Airplanes need two forces to fly—thrust and lift. Four engines thrust this plane forward. The wings lift up the plane.

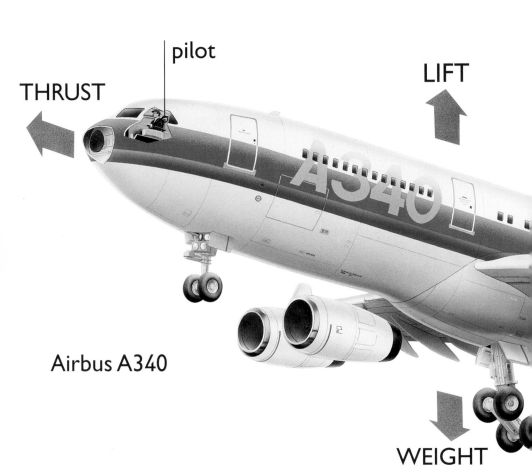

pilot

LIFT

THRUST

Airbus A340

WEIGHT

An Airbus A340 carries many passengers. The plane's weight and drag from the air around it slow the plane down as it flies.

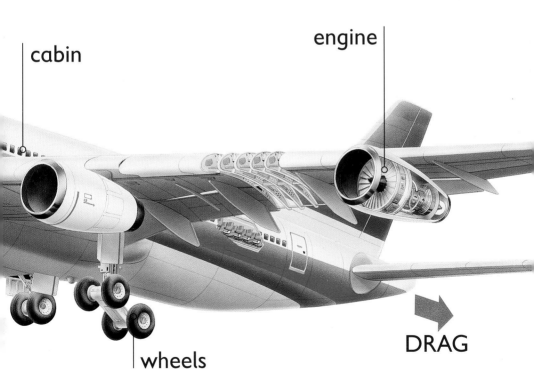

engine

cabin

wheels

DRAG

Scientists use submersibles
to study things in the ocean.

robotic arm

Submersible

Submersibles are undersea vessels.
They use batteries to power propellers
so they can move in all directions. They
can dive underwater to great depths.

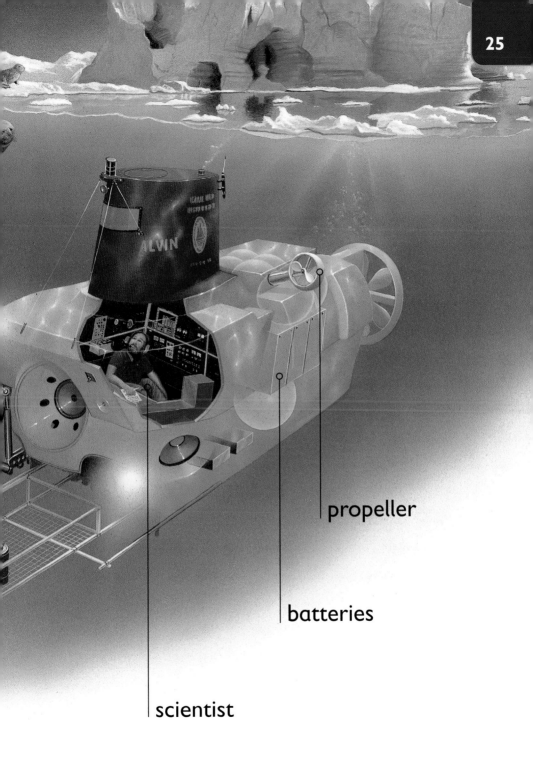

propeller

batteries

scientist

Lock and Key

When a key is put into a lock, it causes a row of tiny metal pins to move. With the correct key, the row of pins will line up to open the lock.

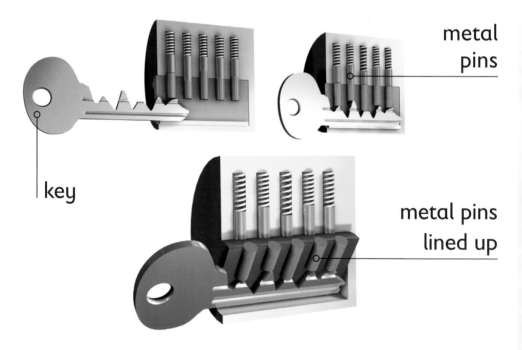

metal pins

key

metal pins lined up

Keys lock and unlock doors. You need the right key to unlock a door.

Radar

A radar transmitter sends out radio waves. It can locate large metal objects such as airplanes. The objects reflect the waves, which bounce back to the transmitter.

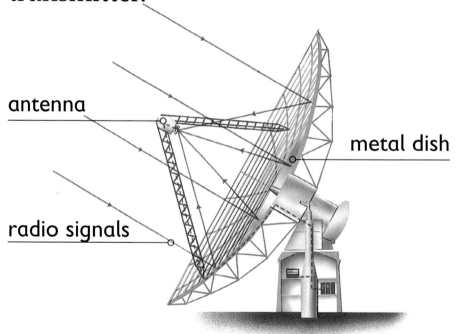

antenna

metal dish

radio signals

A radar transmitter has a metal dish that directs waves into the antenna at the center.

Quiz

Can you match each item with its name?

clock   microwave oven

bicycle   hang glider

Glossary

blades: long, flat parts of a device, such as a windmill

electricity: a form of energy. It can make small lighbulbs, as well as big trains, work.

passengers: people who travel in a vehicle, such as a train or airplane

pedals: levers worked by the feet

pendulum: an object that swings back and forth

propellers: blades that spin around very quickly and pull or push devices

radio waves: waves that carry energy, sounds, or pictures through the air

reflect: to give back an image, as in a mirror

transmitter: a device that sends messages

turntable: the part of a device that revolves

Index